TO GOD BE THE GLORY

CELEBRATING 40 YEARS IN MINISTRY

Dr. Clarence Talley Sr.

WESTBOW
PRESS®
A DIVISION OF THOMAS NELSON
& ZONDERVAN

This book is a work of non-fiction. Unless otherwise noted, the author and the publisher make no explicit guarantees as to the accuracy of the information contained in this book and in some cases, names of people and places have been altered to protect their privacy.

WestBow Press books may be ordered through booksellers or by contacting:

WestBow Press
A Division of Thomas Nelson & Zondervan
1663 Liberty Drive
Bloomington, IN 47403
www.westbowpress.com
844-714-3454

Scripture quotations marked KJV are from the Holy Bible, King James Version (Authorized Version). First published in 1611. Quoted from the KJV Classic Reference Bible, Copyright © 1983 by The Zondervan Corporation.

Holy Bible, New International Version®, NIV® Copyright ©1973, 1978, 1984, 2011 by Biblica, Inc.® Used by permission. All rights reserved worldwide.

ISBN: 979-8-3850-2155-0 (sc)

Library of Congress Control Number: 2024905574

Print information available on the last page.

WestBow Press rev. date: 4/9/2024

CONTENTS

EPIGRAPH

"You don't have to have a college degree to serve. You don't have to make your subject and verb agree to serve. You don't have to know about Plato and Aristotle to serve. You don't have to know about Einstein theory of relativity to serve. You don't have to know the second theory of thermos-dynamics in physics to serve. You only need a heart full of grace. A soul generated by love."

—Martin L. King, Jr.

To
Carolyn, Clarence, Crystal
and the
Mount Corinth Family
and to all the
Churches in Heavenly Hempstead

THE LORD IS MY SHEPHERD

The Lord is my Shepherd. He provides all I need.
A family, a job, and opportunities to do good deeds.

I never have to worry or beg for seeds.
I simply rest in pastures He has designed for me.

In His bosom I lay,
And with renewed passion, I stay.

I follow Him through the hallway of time.
And when I come to a dark valley, I gladly resign.

Though the shadow be dark and deep,
The comfort I need, He provides for me.

For my Shepherd has conquered death, hell, and the grave.
And I am sure I will be raised.

At the table of blessings is where I sit.
With my enemies looking on in discontent.

Exceedingly blessed with whatever I need.
My Lord, My God does nothing but please.

Friends I have; goodness and mercy are their names.
They are always with me; they never change.

In the house of my God, I look forward to stay,
Not just on tomorrow but forever and a day. Amen!
—Clarence Talley, Sr.

PREFACE

Forty years in the ministry is the motivation for this anniversary volume. It is my way of saying *Thank You!* to *my* Shepherd. And I have chosen David's Psalm as my launching pad to express my love and commitment to God because I know, like David, God is my Shepherd and He is committed to me. For forty years, the Lord has shepherded me through His Word so that I might be a light to others and an under-shepherd to His people. Thus, I have chosen to celebrate this milestone by remembering how God stepped in and chose my voice to be His voice.

My testimony to my church family, Mount Corinth Missionary Baptist, has always centers around a childhood incident while singing in the choir. Something amazing happened. This should have been pre-teen. As I sang with others, I began to feel a presence that I've never felt before. We were singing *"I Was Sinking Deep in Sin."* As I looked around, I wondered were the other kids feeling what I felt. Were they experiencing what I was experiencing. I didn't take a poll that day, but since that day life has never been the same.

An old song that the old church used to sing regularly sums up my youthful experience. The title is *My God is Real* better known as *Yes, God is Real.* The first verse reads: *There are some things I may not know, There are some places I can't go, But I am sure of this one thing, That God is real for I can feel Him deep within.*

There have been many years since God's initial contact that eventful day. And the Lord has been my shepherd all along the way. His goodness and His mercy elevated me into the ministry in the early eighties and then to pastoral leadership in 2013. And as a result, I have been proclaiming His goodness ever since.

This book seeks to share my beginnings in the ministry. Thus, I begin with a Prologue and Revelation. The book is not a biography. It is an intimate look at the move of God in calling me to the ministry.

The first chapter title: *A Call From God* is a sermonic chapter with preface, prologue, and postscript is shared in its original form as preached forty years ago. It's personal, revealing, and somewhat rough around the edges. Yet, it reveals the Shepherd's hand in my nervous start.

The remaining chapters/messages are meant to encourage and enlighten beginning with *Driving Directions: How To Get To Restoration Drive*. It is a look at being spiritually lost and what's involved in finding one's way. The life of the prodigal son helps us to do that.

Chapter three: *Honoring Dr. Martin L. King, Jr.* is a sermonic/speech celebrating America's hero. It warns America and the world of the work we still must do to achieve brotherhood. As Dr. King has so forcefully said, "either we live together as brothers or die together as fools."

Chapter four: *Do Your Job* reminds gospel ministers of the awesome responsibility of pastoral leadership and how to be effective in these latter-days. It cautions pastors to stick to the biblical script because the Lord is watching and will evaluate our service.

Chapter five: *Today Is All We Have* stresses the importance of wisely using the time that God has allotted us. The fragility of life and its uncertainties are set before us. And finally, chapter six: *Don't Waste Your Time* further supports chapter five by discussing the value of time well-used.

Again this book is a celebration of God's glory as shown in my ministry. It is meant to say *Thank You!* to Him who is my Shepherd.

To God Be The Glory!

PROLOGUE AND REVELATION

The following is a prologue and revelation to first my first sermon preached under the tutelage of Rev. J. Roland Hicks then Pastor of Mount Corinth Missionary Baptist Church, Hempstead, Texas. I was surrounded by loving church family members and friends who encouraged me with their amens and their halleluiahs. The prologue first appeared in my book: *A Call From God*.

∾

First giving honor to God, Pastor Hicks for his kind introduction, to the officers, members, and friends of Mount Corinth, indeed it is a pleasure to stand before you. This may come as a surprise to some who have known me over the years. But I see this day as the fulfillment of God's will.

Quite often I heard Pastor Hicks and others say, "When you are born, your work is born with you. All that we need to succeed or fail in life enters the world at the moment of birth. Our love, hopes, anguish, doubts, and fears flow through the birth canal and into this cold, cold, world."

God's plan for our lives plus our choices equal the sum total of our contributions to life. God ordains life and He allows us to choose the direction we desire to take. Therefore, I come declaring what God has ordained and planned for my life. He has called and I must answer.

∾

At my residence, on Thursday, January 19, 1984, during the noon hour, I stopped for a moment of prayer. As I prayed, I could feel the Spirit of God stirring in my heart. I realized, then, I could hold out no longer. It was at that very moment, I decided to answer God's call.

Earlier on April 23, 1982, approximately 3:00 a. m. God showed me in a dream, as He had before, what He wanted me to do. I awoke crying and utterly disturbed. Afterwards, I arose and penned the following words:

- The Lord God wants me to preach.
- To spread his word to all.
- At this very moment I am afraid.
- I lack confidence.
- But with God all things are possible.

I am taking time to chronicle this event, because I know this is what God wants me to do. In my dream, God revealed the course I must take. I could see myself standing behind a pulpit, preaching. I could not determine what church pulpit I stood in. I was aware that I was in the presence of friends and loved ones.

I knew that God had spoken to my heart, and I realized what He wants me to do. However, I am afraid that I would not be able to meet the challenge. There was a burning sensation in my heart with words from God. At that point I asked God to give me the wisdom to do His will.

Later, I informed my wife about my experience and decision to preach. We shared tears of joy and gladness as I explained to her that it was God's plan for our lives.

Finally, I informed Rev. Hicks. I chose not to call him and discuss it over the telephone because that seemed so impersonal. Therefore, I waited to tell him on my next visit to his home. I did not expect him to be surprised, because on a number of occasions he had told me that I'll have to preach before I die.

When I told Rev. Hicks, he paused for a moment seemingly to contemplate. Then he asked, "are you sure." I said yes and I asked what I should do next. Rev. Hicks said many things; but the one most important thing was to be prayerful—to always pray.

Several weeks later, Rev. Hicks informed me that the first Sunday, March 4, 1984, would be set aside for me to preach my first sermon. I prepared as best I could. And left the outcome to God.

REVELATION and confirmation occurred on that day. And I recall it vividly.

As I walked to the pulpit from the choir stand on that unforgettable Sunday, March 4, 1984, I had not, in recent days, thought much of the dream which God used to call me, but as I proceeded to the to the pulpit, someone spoke to me. Looking back, I know the voice was that of the Spirit. He said, "Look at yourself." And as I did, a flashback of my initial dream came to me like a bolt of lightning. I had not considered this little detail that in my dream I was dressed in a robe: that's right a robe. From those few steps between the choir stand and the pulpit, the Lord spoke again. The robe was a revelation.

What more confirmation did I need? None! Absolutely none!

A CALL FROM GOD

Everyone is called upon at some time to serve in a specific duty or function. Oftentimes, this makes us feel wanted and even appreciated. An educator may be called upon to serve on a panel to discuss the escalation of violence in our schools and determine what can be done about it.

A scientist may be called upon to devise a plan to conquer world hunger. A medical doctor may be called to the scene of a life-or-death situation. And at the same time, a child may be called upon by its parents to run a simple errand.

No matter how often we are called upon to serve, there is no greater call to serve than "A Call From God."

> *Now Moses kept the flock of Jethro his father in law, the priest of Midian: and he led the flock to the backside of the desert, and came to the mountain of God, even to Horeb. And the angel of the LORD appeared unto him in a flame of fire out of the midst of a bush: and he*

looked, and, behold, the bush burned with fire, and the bush was not consumed.

And Moses said, I will now turn aside, and see this great sight, why the bush is not burnt. And when the LORD saw that he turned aside to see, God called unto him out of the midst of the bush, and said, Moses, Moses. And he said, Here am I. (Exodus 3:1-4 KJV)

Moses is perhaps the most well-known, the most illustrious, and the most majestic figure in the Old Testament. He is credited with writing the first five books of the Bible known as the Torah. The book of Exodus, in which our text is found, presents a dramatic account of Israel's departure from Egypt under the human leadership of Moses and the divine leadership of God,

At the time of Moses birth, the nation of Israel had grown from seventy out of the house of Jacob up to nearly two million souls in the land of Egypt. (Exodus 1:5)

Now that the children of Israel had increased abundantly and the land was filled with them, Pharaoh feared them because they were more and mightier than the Egyptians (Exodus 1:9). As a result, the Pharaoh issued a royal decree and thus had the nation of Israel enslaved. He also ordered the slaughter of all male babies by throwing them into the Nile River. (Exodus 1:16)

It was against this backdrop that Moses was born, and through divine providence, he was spared death and enslavement.

Moses was raised in the house of the Pharaoh and in a testimony by Stephen in Acts 7:22, the young preacher acknowledges that Moses was educated in all the wisdom of the Egyptians and was powerful in speech and action.

Notwithstanding, the stench and the oppression of the Hebrew nation would not leave Moses. Although he lived in the big house, ate the best of foods, slept on the finest linen, had servants at his command and concubines to satisfy his every desire, Moses could not turn his back on his people. And although Moses had riches, splendor, power, and fame, he still chose to identify with the suffering and afflictions of God's people, rather than to enjoy the pleasures of sin for a season. (Hebrew 11:25)

> And although Moses had riches, splendor, power, and fame, he still chose to identify with the suffering and afflictions of God's people, rather than to enjoy the pleasures of sin for a season. (Hebrew 11:25)

Sometimes, we set aside all principles and morals for a fleeting moment of worldly pleasures. We not only forsake God, but we turn our backs on mother, father, sister, brother, neighbor, friend, and even spouse for the pleasures of sin for a season. Moses, however, chose to identify with his people—the nation of Israel—the children of God.

One day, Moses witnessed an Egyptian cruelly beating a Hebrew. He was so enraged that he stepped in and killed the Egyptian and buried him in the sand. (Exodus 2:12) Afraid that his deed would soon reach the ears of the Pharaoh, Moses fled. His flight ended in the land of Midian (Exodus 2:15) And there Moses married into the family of Jethro and became a sheepherder.

Little did Moses know that his run from the Pharaoh was a race toward God. Little did Moses know that he was heeding God's call.

> *Now Moses kept the flock of Jethro his father in law, the priest of Midian: and he led the flock to the backside of the desert, and came to the mountain of God, even to Horeb.* (Exodus 3:1 KJV)

For Moses, this day did not appear to be any different from and other day. Like most sheepherders, Moses went about doing his daily chores. Once a fiery forty years of age, when he slew the Egyptian, now Moses was the ripe age of eighty. Over the last forty years, he had become a humble vessel shaped to the point that God can now use him to deliver His people.

With the passing of time, the fourth generation had arisen in Egypt, and the fulfillment of God's promise to Abraham quietly approached. Meanwhile, the humble and contrite Moses was in the proper position and condition to hear from God. Oftentimes, we make it difficult to be in the right frame of mind to hear from God.

Thus, it takes a whole lot of effort on our part. As in most cases, the hustle and bustle of society easily detract us and draw us away from the voice of God. We must fight to position ourselves against the ways of the world in order to hear from God.

We must keep our loins girded with truth and our lamps filled with oil—God's Word. We've got to drown out the world in order to heed the small still voice of God. Then, like Moses, we will be in a position to hear from God, respond to God, and be used by God.

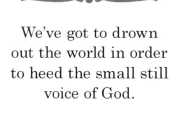

We've got to drown out the world in order to heed the small still voice of God.

And the angel of the LORD appeared unto him in a flame of fire out of the midst of a bush: and he looked, and, behold, the bush burned with fire, and the bush was not consumed. (Exodus 3:2 KJV)

This says to me that God initiated contact with Moses in His own way and time. It is important to understand that God is seeking Moses. This has always been God's mode of operation. After they sinned, Adam and Eve did not seek God. The Lord called unto Adam, and said unto him, "Where art thou?" We don't discover God; He reveals Himself to us. And as the Spirit of God reveals Himself to His elect, we are drawn by His divine presence. For Moses, it was the glow of the bush that attracted his attention.

Today, God is still trying to get mankind's attention, but many refuse to look upon the burning bush of His Word. Many have their eyes focused on the wrong things or person. Some are watching their friends, neighbor, and or relatives. Many are following the crowd instead of the brilliant light of Jesus Christ. He is still the light on which every eye should focus.

The prophet Isaiah had his eyes focused on the stability, prosperity, and peacefulness of King Uzziah's reign. It was not until the king died that Isaiah could truly see the Lord and recognize God's plan for his life. (Isaiah 6)

Isaiah was not seeking or expecting a call from God when he went into the temple, Isaiah 6. But there he saw God sitting on the throne "high and lifted up." Isaiah did not expect to hear God ask, "Whom shall we send, and who will go for us." Yet, Isaiah boldly responded, "Here am I; send me." God initiated the call, but Isaiah had to respond.

The prophet Ezekial was another who was not expecting to be called. He went out one day and sat down by the River Chebar. He was sitting there contemplating the plight of his nation Judah who was now in Babylonian captivity. When, suddenly, the Lord appeared to him in the midst of an awesome storm cloud. Ezekial responded but God initiated the call.

In Jeremiah 1:5, God tells the young Jeremiah, *Before I formed thee in the belly I knew thee; and before thou camest forth out of the womb I sanctified thee, and I ordained thee a prophet unto the nations* (KJV). Long before Jeremiah could respond, God had initiated the call for him to tear down, to build, and to destroy.

The prophetical call of Isaiah, Ezekial, and Jeremiah all demonstrate unequivocally that God seeks out men to use according to His will and purpose. He alone knows who is needed and whom He has equipped to do the job. Once the call is initiated there has to be a response or reaction to the call whether negative or positive. For example, when the telephone or doorbell rings, we must first hear the ring before we can respond. Afterwards, the decision is made whether to answer or not to answer.

Moses replied, *I will now turn aside and see this great sight and learn why the bush is not burnt,* (Exodus 3:3 KJV). The burning bush aroused the curiosity of Moses. His inquisitive spirit wanted to know the mystery of the burning bush. Little did Moses know, however, that the lure of the burning bush was a call from the almighty God.

Certainly the call of Moses was no ordinary call. The call was made to a man who suckled his mother's breast, was turned over to the Pharaoh's daughter, was schooled by Egyptian professors, and was brought to the desert to be commissioned by God.

Certainly, this was no ordinary call; it was specifically designed and tailored for Moses. He did not seek it nor did he want it.

~

I say to you there is nothing you or I can do to earn favor or a call from God. No man chooses this profession; the divine Employer selects the man. In His divine wisdom, the great God of the universe stamps His seal of approval on the call after which it is delivered by an angel of the Lord.

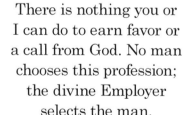

There is nothing you or I can do to earn favor or a call from God. No man chooses this profession; the divine Employer selects the man.

- There is no application to fill out.
- No waiting list to sign-up on.
- No employment office to visit.

- You don't need a social security number.
- No special plan of education.
- You don't need a street address.
- A post office box or a telephone number.

Just bear in mind: God calls whom He desires—anybody, anytime, anywhere. He does not use Bell Telephone or AT&T. The divine call is placed from the bosom of God to the hearts of willing and unwilling servants.

As I close the question come to mind: when He calls will you answer? God is calling for the:

- Young and the old
- High and the low
- Rich and the poor
- Learned and the unlearned
- Careless and the indifferent

Will you take up your cross and follow Jesus? Will you forsake all and heed God's call? Whosoever will, let him come.

Mose answered the call and challenged the Pharaoh of Egypt.
John the Baptist answered the call and introduced Jesus to the world.
Isaiah answered the call and was sent to warn the nation of Israel.
Paul, formerly Saul, answered the call and was sent unto the Gentiles.
James and John answered the call and became fishers of men.
Peter answered the call and was given the keys to the kingdom.

A Call From God…. Will You Answer?

NOTES

NOTES

DRIVING DIRECTIONS:
HOW TO GET TO
RESTORATION DRIVE

When we find ourselves lost, it's crucial to pause and seek assistance. Continuing along the same path while being lost only exacerbates the situation. What's even worse, though, than being lost, is not realizing that you are lost, as this ignorance keeps the door to help firmly shut.

Without God, man is spiritually adrift, unable to find his way on his own. Man lacks the inclination to seek God's guidance. The apostle Paul emphasizes that we are all sinners and that "there is no one who understands, no one who seeks God" (Romans 3:11b, 23 NIV).

> Without God, man is spiritually adrift, unable to find his way on his own.

Without the guidance of the Holy Spirit, man lacks the necessary directions, wisdom, and spiritual navigation to return to God, to find the straight and narrow path leading back to Him. Consequently, God had to provide a roadmap for our return.

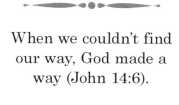

> When we couldn't find our way, God made a way (John 14:6).

When we couldn't find our way, God made a way (John 14:6). "While we were yet sinners, Christ died for us" (Romans 5:8 KJV). Through Jesus Christ's death, burial, and resurrection, the way to restoration is now accessible. We have directions for our journey back.

In Luke 15:11 through 24, we find an excellent example of a young man who lost his way by heading in the wrong direction. He traveled down various streets, freeways, turnpikes, and alleys before finally finding the path to restoration.

The story is filled with twists, sharp curves, speed bumps, and potholes that should have served as warnings. The Lord often uses such obstacles to caution us, wake us up, slow us down, and redirect us toward the road leading to Him.

In Luke 15:11-12, we witness a young man leaving his father's house, convinced that his chosen direction was justified and necessary. However, prior to leaving his father's house, this young man was entirely self-centered. He was headed for Selfish Street. Listen to his request:

"There was a man who had two sons. The younger one said to his father, 'Father, give me my share of the estate.' So, he divided his property between them" (NIV).

Selfish Street is a path not taken by accident. Usually, when we venture down this street, we are fully aware of it. We utter phrases like "it's my way or no way," "I'm grown, I can make my own decisions," or "it's my thing, I do what I want to do." On Selfish

Street, our thoughts are consumed by self-interest. We echo Frank Sinatra's sentiment, singing, "I Did It My Way."

On Selfish Street, neither mama nor daddy can sway us. In fact, on Selfish Street, even God's words fall on deaf ears with hardened hearts. Here, one's focus is solely on themselves.

Listen to the prodigal son as he selfishly claims his independence, saying, "Father, give me my share of the estate." So, the father divided his property between them.

The prodigal son hasn't experienced much of the world yet, but he makes an audacious demand. His basic needs, such as food, clothing, and shelter, were all provided for by his father. He is still inexperienced, yet he insists on claiming his share of the estate. What had he accumulated to call his own?

It's worth noting that the father never engages in a conversation with the boy, at least not according to the text. He simply divides his property between the younger son and the older brother. Scholars have concluded that the father symbolizes our heavenly Father – all-wise, all-knowing, eternally giving, and forgiving.

The text doesn't explicitly mention it, but surely the father's heart aches. No doubt, the father had dreams and aspirations for his son, much like God does for us. Dreams of seeing his son achieve heights that he himself had not reached – not just in terms of material wealth, but morally, intellectually, socially, and spiritually. Nevertheless, it's essential to remember that God has granted humanity free will – a boundary even our heavenly Father respects. "So he divided his property between them."

> Remember that God has granted humanity free will – a boundary even our heavenly Father respects.

The old proverb, "be careful what you ask for, because you just might get it," comes to mind. The father grants his son's wish, and he sets out on his own – free, determined to be self-reliant, and above all, materially satisfied.

Next, in verse 13, we see the young man taking a detour onto the Party Hardy Freeway.

Be careful what you ask for, because you just might get it.

"Not long after that, the younger son gathered all he had, journeyed to a distant country, and there wasted his wealth in wild living" (Luke 15:13 NIV).

The Party Hardy Freeway leads the young man away from God and away from his father's house, taking him to a place referred to as a 'distant country.' This freeway leads to a realm where good times roll around the clock. Day and night, he indulges in eating, drinking, merrymaking, womanizing, and lavish spending with newfound friends. In those times, the distant country could have easily been places like Carthage, Alexandria, Antioch, or Rome, enticing those who seek to squander their health and wealth.

Today, the Party Hardy Freeway leads to hotspots like the Las Vegas Strip, the French Quarter in New Orleans, and gambling casinos in Louisiana, Texas, and Mississippi.

The distant country doesn't necessarily refer to far-off lands; it can encompass any space or separation between a person and God. Anything that comes between you and God, whether it's a person, place, thing, or thought, places you in the

Anything that comes between you and God, whether it's a person, place, thing, or thought, places you in the distant country. It's not about physical distance or location; it's about spiritual disconnection.

distant country. It's not about physical distance or location; it's about spiritual disconnection. It's about the state of your relationship with God. When our choices lead us away from the right path, we find ourselves in a distant country.

The prodigal son's recklessness and stubbornness took him away from his father's house and thrust him into a world for which he was unprepared. On the Party Hardy Freeway, he ventured his own way, forgetting the warning that "there is a way that seems right to a man, but its end is the way to death." Regrettably, he squandered the blessings his father had bestowed on him through unrighteous living.

One of life's certainties teaches us that we can never predict what tomorrow holds. The prodigal son learned this lesson the hard way as he squandered everything he had. It's important to note that he was now penniless.

"After he had spent everything, there was a severe famine in the whole country, and he began to be in need." (Luke 15:14 NIV)

Now the prodigal found himself on Penniless Lane – broke, shattered, and disheartened. On Penniless Lane, you're not just down to your last dime; you have no dime at all. The prodigal had spent everything, and it wasn't on tithes and offerings; it was squandered in pursuit of worldly pleasures.

> The prodigal had spent everything, and it wasn't on tithes and offerings.

Indulging in eating, drinking, and merrymaking without considering God will always leave you penniless. Trying to satisfy yourself and others through worldly means will lead to financial ruin. Neglecting to save for a rainy day (like the severe famine in that country) can leave you without resources. Living beyond your means can render you homeless, friendless, and penniless.

Now, in desperate need and unable to meet his basic necessities, the prodigal embarked on the Hogpen Turnpike.

"So he went and hired himself out to a citizen of the country, who sent him to his fields to feed pigs." (Luke 15:15 NIV)

Far from home and lacking the means to support himself, he took a degrading job tending swine. An Israelite noble, raised in a loving home with a caring father, was now reduced to tending pigs. Even at his lowest point in the distant country, the thought of returning home had not yet crossed his mind. And even if it did, could he make it from the hog pen to his father's house on Restoration Drive? That remains to be seen.

The prodigal's situation had now become dire. He was homeless, helpless, and hungry, with no immediate solution in sight.

"He longed to fill his stomach with the pods that the pigs were eating, but no one gave him anything." (Luke 15:16 NIV)

Amid a barren place, the prodigal's stomach starts to rumble. No more feasts with lamb chops, wine, and fresh bread. No one left to offer him the crumbs from their tables. Gradually, the swine's slop begins to appear appetizing to the young man. With mud-caked feet, pig filth on his hands, and a longing for their food in his heart, the prodigal hits rock bottom.

These conditions prompt the prodigal to reevaluate his situation, leading him to Recognition Boulevard. Listen to his awakening:

"When he came to his senses, he said, 'How many of my father's hired servants have food to spare, and here I am starving to death.'" (Luke 15:17 NIV)

In another translation, it's put as "And when he came to himself." On Recognition Boulevard, the prodigal makes a resolute decision to return to his father. He finally comprehends the extent of his foolishness. His father had resources to employ and care for numerous servants, yet he himself was starving—servants enjoyed warm beds, hearty meals (even showers and big-screen TVs). No one in his father's house lacked for anything, but he had been deprived of it all.

⸺ ◆●◆ ⸺

In the hog pen, the prodigal recognizes the gravity of his errors. His aching heart takes him on a journey down memory lane.

⸺ ◆●◆ ⸺

In the hog pen, the prodigal recognizes the gravity of his errors. His aching heart takes him on a journey down memory lane. He realizes that poverty, estrangement from his father, and weariness of the soul need not be his fate.

From Recognition Boulevard, the prodigal's path of repentance leads him to Confession Avenue. Confession Avenue is where we all must arrive to restore our right relationship with our heavenly Father. Therefore, the prodigal sincerely confesses, saying:

"I will set out and go back to my father and say to him: Father, I have sinned against heaven and against you. I am no longer worthy to be called your son; make me like one of your hired servants." (Luke 15:18-19 NIV)

Recognition, confession, and repentance set the prodigal on the road to his father's house, specifically on Restoration Drive. Determined to return home, he rehearses his speech carefully, wasting no time bidding farewell to his former life. He understands that home is where he belongs, and so he sets his course homeward.

As the reunion draws near, the father spots his son from a distance, leading to a touching and affectionate scene. Our heavenly Father sees us both up close and from afar. He knows our every move, our thoughts, and never forgets us, nor does He forsake us. The heavenly

⸺ ◆●◆ ⸺

Our heavenly Father sees us both up close and from afar. He knows our every move, our thoughts, and never forgets us, nor does He forsake us.

⸺ ◆●◆ ⸺

Father eagerly awaits our return. Thus, the prodigal heads back to the father, albeit with a sense of shame.

"So he got up and went to his father. But while he was still a long way off, his father saw him and was filled with compassion for him; he ran to his son, threw his arms around him and kissed him. The son said to him, 'Father, I have sinned against heaven and against you. I am no longer worthy to be called your son.' But the father said to his servants, 'Quick! Bring the best robe and put it on him. Put a ring on his finger and sandals on his feet. Bring the fattened calf and kill it. Let's have a feast and celebrate. For this son of mine was dead and is alive again; he was lost and is found.' So they began to celebrate." (Luke 15:20-24 NIV)

Dirty, smelling, with a confession on his lips and repentance in his soul, the young man returns to a home and a father whose open arms of forgiveness welcome him back wholeheartedly. To have his son back, unharmed, is a joyous occasion, an answered prayer, and a reason to celebrate. The son is restored, and the father is overjoyed. Orders are given to prepare for a grand feast. What was lost has now been found.

We all must seek directions to Restoration Drive, the home of the father's house. And when we do, we'll realize that the father awaits us all. Understanding that we have all sinned, we must confess and seek to reunite with our heavenly Father.

Life's journey may take you through Selfish Street, onto Party Hardy Freeway, and down Penniless Lane. You might even find yourself on the Hogpen Turnpike at an all-time low. The turnpike is a rough road leading only to a place with no food and no friends.

After all the twists, turns,

> Confession accompanied by repentance will lead you to Restoration Drive, to a renewed relationship with God, and to your heavenly home.

and dead ends you may have encountered, hopefully, like the prodigal, you've come to realize that there is a better way, and it starts with confession (Romans 10:9). Surely, confession accompanied by repentance will lead you to Restoration Drive, to a renewed relationship with God, and to your heavenly home.

NOTES

NOTES

HONORING DR. MARTIN L. KING, JR.

Dr. Martin Luther King Jr. Day in America, celebrated worldwide, is a day to honor Dr. King for his relentless efforts to create a better world. This honor is well-deserved.

Dr. King was a remarkable preacher, a devout man of God, a champion of freedom, a husband, a father, an exceptional orator, and a catalyst for change. We pause to celebrate his life and the invaluable contributions he made. We owe him a debt of gratitude for his sacrifices.

Born into a family of preachers, Dr. King's grandfather, Rev. A. D. Williams, and Martin Luther King Sr., both served as pastors at the Ebenezer Baptist Church in Atlanta, Georgia. The calling to preach ran deep in his blood. Initially, ministry was not his first choice; he initially aspired to become a doctor, lawyer, or university president before embracing the highest calling—disciple of Jesus Christ, communicator of the gospel, and a voice speaking out against racial and economic injustices.

Dr. King wasn't just a disciple; he was a proponent of nonviolence in his pursuit of leveling the playing field and ensuring every individual's recognition of their God-given, inalienable rights. To achieve this, he chose nonviolence as his weapon.

While some around him advocated for different approaches like indifference, violence, or "by any means necessary," Dr. King steadfastly followed the teachings of the Bible, particularly "love your enemies, bless them that curse you, do good to them that hate you, and pray for them that despitefully use you." While the world might have preferred "burn, baby, burn," Dr. King championed "learn, baby, learn, build, baby, build, earn, baby, earn."

> While the world might have preferred "burn, baby, burn," Dr. King championed "learn, baby, learn, build, baby, build, earn, baby, earn."

Dr. King integrated the teachings of Jesus Christ, the philosophy of Henry David Thoreau (who advocated "civil disobedience to an unjust state"), and the methods of Mahatma Gandhi. This synthesis led to Dr. King's unique approach of nonviolent action to achieve specific political and social goals. He explained his approach by saying, "Christ furnished the spirit and motivation, while Gandhi furnished the method."

As a young pastor fresh out of Morehouse College, Crozer Theological Seminary, and Boston University, Dr. King found himself at the forefront of the Civil Rights movement following Rosa Parks' refusal to give up her seat on a racially segregated bus on December 1, 1955, which led to her arrest.

Suddenly, this young pastor was thrust into leading a massive movement for social justice. Although largely untested on American soil, nonviolence became Dr. King's means of bridging racial divides. Besides Jesus Christ and nonviolence, he had nothing else to offer. Dr. King's remarkable rise at such a critical time placed him squarely within God's plan for America and the world.

King and his followers, some of whom initially had doubts about his methods, endured threats, arrests, and countless jail cells. Acts of violence, deaths of both black and white individuals, police use of tear gas, nightsticks, guns, water hoses, and police dogs were met with remarkably peaceful demonstrations, boycotts, and sit-ins.

In a speech after Dr. King's arrest during the Montgomery boycott, he urged his audience to stay the course, emphasizing the importance of nonviolence. He said, "If we are arrested every day, if we are exploited every day, if we are trampled over every day, don't ever let anyone pull you so low as to hate them." Dr. King insisted, "We must use the weapon of love. We must have compassion and understanding for those who hate us. We must realize that many people are taught to hate us and are not responsible for their own hate. But we stand in life at midnight; we are always on the threshold of a new dawn."

> We must use the weapon of love. We must have compassion and understanding for those who hate us.

Nonviolence, rooted in a Christian worldview, kept the concept of brotherhood in the forefront. To Dr. King, it was never about Black versus White because all individuals were valuable in the eyes of God. He believed that "an individual has value because he has value to God. Whenever this is recognized, whiteness and blackness pass away." This vision was vividly articulated in his "I have a Dream" speech, where he dreamt of a day when his children would be judged by their character, not by the color of their skin.

Dr. King emphasized that "to gain rights for Negroes without mainstream America desiring the same would have been a shallow and unsustainable victory." For Dr. King, the movement was about love, justice, and brotherhood, leaving no room for hatred, injustice, or enmity.

During his acceptance speech for the Nobel Peace Prize in 1964, Dr. King proclaimed that "the oceans of history are made turbulent by the ever-rising tides of hate. History is cluttered with the wreckage of nations and

> For Dr. King, the movement was about love, justice, and brotherhood, leaving no room for hatred, injustice, or enmity.

individuals that pursued that self-defeating path of hate." He argued that "love is the key to the solution of the problems of the world."

Engaging in violence against one's brothers and sisters tears apart the fabric of brotherhood, a fabric that every person is woven into, regardless of race, creed, or color. Dr. King asserted that "violence, as a way of achieving racial justice, is both impractical and immoral. It is impractical because it is a descending spiral ending in destruction for all. The old law of an eye for an eye leaves everybody blind. It is immoral because it seeks to humiliate the opponent rather than win his understanding; it seeks to annihilate rather than convert.

> While Dr. King tragically fell victim to violence through an assassin's bullet, it is not the violence that lingers in our hearts and memories.

Violence is immoral because it thrives on hatred rather than love. It destroys community and makes brotherhood impossible."

Dr. Martin Luther King, a practitioner of nonviolence, demonstrated to the world the power of peaceful, non-aggressive methods. While Dr. King tragically fell victim to violence through an assassin's bullet, it is not the violence that lingers in our hearts and memories. It's not the stabbings in New York, the stonings in Chicago, or even the assassination in Memphis.

Today, we come together to commemorate a man who, with God's grace, made a profound impact during his lifetime. His dream, more than six decades later, still captivates a world grappling with seemingly insurmountable social and economic challenges, political conflicts, and moral decay.

This day is a celebration of the man, his movement, and his message. Most importantly, we gather to remind ourselves and the world that Dr. Martin Luther King Jr.'s work is far from finished. It endures because it is God's work. It persists until God's will prevails on earth as it does in heaven. It endures because the Lord continues to "trample out the vintage where the grapes of wrath are stored; He hath loosed the fateful lightning of His terrible swift sword." It endures because God's truth marches on.

Though Dr. King is no longer with us, the world still grapples with issues like poverty, racism, prejudice, and more. We still face inhumanity through hate crimes, unjust laws, and judicial injustices. Random acts of gun violence, shootings in public places, and domestic violence underscore the long road ahead.

Greed remains prevalent, homeownership is elusive, and the cost of essentials puts a strain on average families. Beyond our borders, wars and conflicts persist, nations are at odds with one another, and the world faces new challenges like COVID and natural disasters.

Amid family conflicts and divisions, the work is far from over. Today, let us remember that the mission remains unaccomplished, and the case is still open. In the words of Robert Frost, "we still have miles to go before we sleep." People of all races and backgrounds must recognize the urgency of the work and take action now.

To emphasize the urgency of the moment and the responsibility that none of us can delay, Jesus told His disciples, "I must work the works of him that sent me, while it is day: for night cometh, when no man can work." Dr. King lived out this declaration. He worked tirelessly, knowing that night would eventually come. Serving others in accordance with God's will kept him going.

King's philosophical teachings, nonviolent movement, and powerful proclamation of God's Word pointed people toward a higher path—the path of brotherhood.

Let us recommit ourselves to doing what we can, when we can, as often as we can, until our time is up. Unlike Dr. King, we may not be on a national or international stage. We may not have a national holiday in our honor, or his oratorical skills, or the prospect of a Nobel Peace Prize. However, we can declare, like the songwriter, "I'm going to work until my day is done. I'm going to work until the setting of the sun. I'll cease from sorrows, there'll be no tomorrow. I'm going to work until my day is done." Rest assured; God will honor your efforts.

> King's philosophical teachings, nonviolent movement, and powerful proclamation of God's Word pointed people toward a higher path—the path of brotherhood.

NOTES

NOTES

DO YOUR JOB

"I charge thee therefore before God, and the Lord Jesus Christ, who shall judge the quick and the dead at his appearing and his kingdom; Preach the word; be instant in season, out of season; reprove, rebuke, exhort with all long suffering and doctrine. For the time will come when they will not endure sound doctrine; but after their own lusts shall they heap to themselves teachers, having itching ears; And they shall turn away their ears from the truth, and shall be turned unto fables. But watch thou in all things, endure afflictions, do the work of an evangelist, make full proof of thy ministry."

2 Timothy 4:1-5 KJV

The Apostle Paul spoke these words to his beloved son Timothy. The occasion for the charge came because of the apostle's imminent departure. Paul would soon be put to death; hence, he takes time to encourage young Timothy regarding his duties as a minister.

His advice to his young son in the ministry was simply to, "Do Your Job." Timothy is cautioned to do his job because God the Father and Son are watching, and at some point in time, at an hour in which no man knows, Jesus Christ will come to judge his work (v. 1).

The charge to Timothy is not just for pastor-preachers; it is also for all Christians. All of us have been assigned a ministry or ministries we are accountable for and are obligated to carry out faithfully before the Master return.

Now, most of us have regular jobs or have worked in some capacity. We know about and understand the responsibilities of having to work for someone. The business is not ours; we are just employed in some capacity. We are the employees, and the owner is the employer. This means we work for the boss; the boss doesn't work for us.

On our earthly jobs, in some way or means, we are watched by the boss or monitored according to his wishes. We may be watched by an immediate supervisor or manager who reports to the boss. Or other mechanisms are used to monitor our arrival and progress, such as time clocks, cameras, and even other

On our earthly jobs, in some way or means, we are watched by the boss or monitored according to his wishes.

co-workers. Whatever method is used to monitor workers, most employees understand they are being watched. From Paul, Timothy receives full warning that the Boss; God the Father and God the Son are watching him execute his office.

On most jobs, when there is a lack of supervision, people will try to get away with doing little or nothing at all. The tendency is to slack off when they think nobody is watching. Timothy, however, was not to slack off; he was to faithfully fulfill his duty. He was encouraged to do his job, be a good steward, a fervent worker, and not give in to slothful behavior (Romans 12:11, Hebrews 6:12a).

Why is this so important? Because one day, Timothy and all who claim to be born again will have to give an account to the Lord who will come and judge the entire world and to set up His kingdom. Those who are alive and those He will call forth from the graves, will all stand before the Lord and give a personal accounting (Matthew 25:31-46; Romans 14:10-12).

Thus Paul urges Timothy, "Since the Boss is watching, you must be ever so careful as an employee of the Lord to faithfully perform the duties for which you have been called and ordained."

No believer will get away with carrying out their assigned duties according to their own desires. And no pastor/leader can lead the church the way they want without consequences. The Boss will not be pleased (Luke 12:42-48).

Why, because in the first place, the church does not belong to the pastor. It belongs to Christ, and it was purchased

> **No pastor/leader can lead the church the way they want without consequences.**

with His blood. The Lord made this plain to Peter and the other disciples, when He said, "Upon this rock I will build my Church" (Matthew 16:18).

Secondly, the pastor is simply the under-shepherd, and Jesus Christ is the chief Shepherd (1 Peter 5:4) and the Good Shepherd (John 10:11). To the church at Ephesus, Paul identifies Jesus as Lord and as the head of the church (Ephesians 5:23). Paul also reminds Timothy that there had been pastors/shepherds that the Lord had watched and was not pleased with their performance.

The Lord watched and evaluated the pastors in Jeremiah's day, pastors that transgressed and walked after things that were worthless. And in those days, God warned:

> Many pastors have destroyed my vineyard, they have trodden my portion under foot, they have made my pleasant portion a desolate wilderness." "Woe be unto the pastors that destroy and scatter the sheep of my pasture! saith the Lord. Therefore thus saith the Lord God of Israel against the pastors that feed my people; Ye have scattered my flock, and driven them away, and have not visited them: behold, I will visit upon you the evil of your doings, saith the Lord (Jeremiah 12:10, 23:1-2 KJV).

Likewise, the Apostle Paul tells his young son to "do what he is told." And by that Paul meant to: "Preach the word be instant in season, out of season; reprove, rebuke, exhort with all long suffering and doctrine" (v. 4:2).

With God as the Employer and Timothy the employee, there was no room to vacillate. Timothy must do what the Boss requires. These requirements, in a sense, were Timothy's job description: to preach, to reprove, to rebuke, and to exhort.

You see, as an employee of Prairie View A&M University, in the Texas A&M University system, my contract outlines my job description under the broad heading of *"terms and conditions."* More specifically, it details my prospective duties as *teaching, research / creative work, and service.* I am also required to comply with all University procedures and regulations. I must do what is required of me. I must follow my job description, especially since my superiors are watching, and at some point, they will evaluate me. More importantly, I want to keep my job and at the first of each month receive my reward.

Knowing that the watchful eye of God was on him, Timothy was charged to "do what he was told" or suffer the consequences of his disobedience. He had to fulfill his job description, which was primarily to *preach the word*. Timothy's supreme task was to preach. He was charged to comply with all aspects of preaching—to reprove, rebuke, and exhort.

Timothy was also charged to recognize the *urgency* of preaching by always being prepared and always looking for an opportunity to share the gospel: to tell someone about the magnificence of the Master.

Like Timothy, we, too, must always be on standby—always ready to exploit opportunities to speak for Jesus Christ. At home, work, in our communities, wherever the Holy Spirit opens the door of opportunity, we are charged to make good use of it.

Timothy was urged to proclaim the saving work through Jesus Christ because man's sinful condition could only be changed by the preached Word. "Faith," what man needs the most, "Cometh by hearing, and hearing by the word of God" (Romans 10:17 KJV). "How shall they hear without a preacher? And how shall they preach except they be sent?" (Romans 10:14c-15a KJV). Timothy's job was to preach what men so desperately needed to hear, and that was, and still is, the Word of God.

There is life in the Word of God. There is hope in the Word of God, and man needs both. Timothy's charge was to, "Preach the word."

Timothy was to follow in the footsteps of other great preachers: like Noah, "preacher of righteousness," (2 Peter 2:5)

> There is life in the Word of God. There is hope in the Word of God, and man needs both.

who preached about *rising water* while proclaiming *the ark of safety*; like Solomon, the wise leader who referred to himself as a preacher who taught the "words of truth" (Ecclesiastes12:9-10); like David, the one-time shepherd boy made King, who declared that he had "preached righteousness in the great congregation" Psalm 40:9); and like Isaiah, the eagle eye prophet who "preached good tidings unto the meek" and thus brought "comfort" to the people of God (61:1, 40:1-2).

The Old Testament preachers, linked with the great messengers of the New Testament, are examples to be emulated: from Jesus, the premier example, to Peter, the Pentecost preacher, to James, the leader of the early church, to John, the revelator, to Phillip, the evangelist and, of course, the Apostle Paul, the planter of Churches and mentor to young Timothy and many others. If Timothy "preached the word" as instructed, he, too, would be numbered among the great heralds of the gospel.

The importance of Timothy's duty to preach is made plain in the phrase to be "instant in season and out of season"; "be urgent in season and out of season," (RSV); and "be prepared in season and out of season" (NIV). Paul charges Timothy to get busy with his duty; preach the gospel.

Paul warned there should be no delay in breaking the grip of Satan and sin in the lives of men—lives that are in ruins, lives that are in search of the narrow path. Being "instant in season and out of season" meant that the young preacher had to take advantage of every situation. Timothy was to be prepared to share the Word of God, whether he felt like it or not, whether he wanted to or not.

The Word of God is not like watermelons, peaches, or tomatoes, which are in one season, and out the next. The Word of God is always in season; it is never inappropriate. It speaks to all situations for all time. It provides hope where there is despair, joy where there is sorrow, and peace where there is chaos. Winter, summer, spring, or fall, the Word of God is in season for all. We, like Timothy,

The Word of God is always in season; it is never inappropriate. It speaks to all situations for all time.

must always be prepared to share the apt and ever-appropriate Word of God.

REPROVE, REBUKE, AND EXHORT

Timothy had to reprove, rebuke, and exhort; these are the specifics of preaching; using them ensures results. To reprove means *to convince, to convict*. In setting forth the gospel, the preacher is to convince, to argue, or to reason by systematically presenting scriptural evidence.

Jesus Christ, for example, skillfully reproved the shrewd and deceitful scribes and Pharisees. He did so on many occasions. One reproof occurred when they brought to Him a woman caught in adultery. They brought her to Jesus to trick and discredit Him. The Lord, however, reproved the scribes and the Pharisees, first with His *silence*, then with His *writing*, and finally by what He *said*.

Jesus declared, "He who is without sin among you, let him throw a stone at her first" (John 8:7 NKJV). As a result, "They heard it, being convicted by their own conscience, went out one by one" (John 8:9ff NKJV). Timothy was also to rebuke those when necessary. In the Greek rebuke means *to set a weight upon*. Timothy was to set the weight of God's Word before the people and on the people. He was not to appease evil and wrongdoing. Timothy was to faithfully lay the weight of right and righteousness upon the people in hope that they would see the error of their ways and change.

Though most people do not like being corrected, it is still the duty of the preacher/pastor to issue firm rebukes to direct people in the path of righteousness, into a closer relationship with God and others.

Jesus Christ had to rebuke Peter, His closest disciple, because he attempted to detour Christ from His appointment at Calvary. In speaking to the demonic influence that was encouraging Peter to challenge His Master, Jesus said: "Out of my sight, Satan! You are a stumbling block to me; you do not have in mind the things of God, but the things of men." Peter needed the firm rebuke from the Master that he may clearly see the error of his way (Matthew 16:21-23 NIV).

The young preacher is also told to exhort. To exhort is to *encourage.* Timothy was to offer words of encouragement in hope that people would courageously walk by faith and thereby become all that God had ordained for their individual lives and the local Church. "Thou shall not" must never be the only message to the people. People also need encouragement. They need to be encouraged to "hang in there" with the Holy Spirit. They need to be encouraged and reminded of the fact that the Lord has promised "never to leave or forsake them" as they wrestle with the complexities and pressures that accompany this life.

> "Thou shall not" must never be the only message to the people. People also need encouragement.

Finally, Timothy was to carry out his preaching duty with *longsuffering,* which is patience, and with *doctrine,* which is teaching. People may not catch on, respond, or turn around as quickly as the preacher would have them to. People may not immediately buy into acting on faith, walking by faith, living by faith. Their growth in grace may not be at a rate that pleases Timothy. Some may not *love* wholeheartedly. Others may not *give* at the level needed to sustain the church. Many may avoid serving in any capacity.

But still, Timothy was to be patient with them. He had to take time and teach those whose faith may be weak, teach those who bear few fruits, teach those who had yet to understand the biblical principles of sacrificial living and giving. So far, the apostle Paul, who was fast approaching death, charged Timothy to do his job as a preacher of the gospel.

Timothy was to be cognizant of the fact that God the Father and God the Son was watching, and one day they would return to judge his work in the ministry (2 Timothy 4:1). Therefore, as a faithful minister, Timothy was to preach the word: lovingly reprove, rebuke, and exhort. Furthermore, always be prepared to speak on God's behalf.

STRIKE THE IRON WHILE IT IS HOT

Now, Paul continues by warning Timothy that he must do his job while the time was right. Paul explained, "For the time will come when they will not endure sound doctrine; but after their own lusts shall they heap to themselves teachers, having itching ears" (2 Timothy 4:3). Ever since man sinned and shamefully exited Paradise, it has been hard for him to endure sound doctrine.

From Adam who literally hid from the Lord to the close of history, there will be those who will turn a deaf ear to the truth which can make them free (Genesis 3:8ff; John 8:32). The period in which Timothy preached had its own share of false teachers, false preachers, and charlatans, but here Paul speaks of a far worst time: for a time is coming when men would rather hear everything except the Word of God.

In chapter three of this same book, 2 Timothy, Paul warns Timothy, "That in the last days perilous times shall come. For men shall be lovers of their own selves…Having a form of godliness, but denying the power thereof." Paul then gives a whole litany of evil characteristics and activities that will plague the Church in the last days. He says:

> People will be lovers of themselves, lovers of money, boastful, proud, abusive, disobedient to their parents, ungrateful, unholy, without love, unforgiving, slanderous, without self-control,

brutal, not lovers of the good, treacherous, rash, conceited, lovers of pleasure rather than lovers of God (vv. 2-4 NIV).

With so much evil on the horizon, Paul wanted Timothy to know it was time to boldly declare the Word. Timothy must strike the iron while it is hot. Timothy was to do all he could while he could; for the time was coming when good wholesome preaching would be rejected.

Instead of swallowing a good dose of God's Word, which is sound doctrine, people "after their own lusts shall they heap to themselves teachers, having itching ears." They would prefer teachers who would scratch their itch by telling them what they wanted to hear rather than applying the balm of the Gospel to their wretched condition. Remember Paul is talking about church folk. Although they refused to listen to the word of God, they would not leave the church either.

Instead, these members would stay in the church, and they wanted things their way. They wanted to play church. They would heap to themselves teachers; in other words, they would selfishly collect or gather teachers who would do what they wanted; pastor/teachers who followed rather than lead; teachers who were made in their own image; teachers who would not hold reproving, rebuking, and exhorting in high esteem.

The time Paul warns about was coming. It would be a time when congregations would seek pastors/teachers that would preach and teach according to the congregation's wishes and dictates. The congregation would rather forget about Jeremiah 3:15 and hire pastor/teachers who followed the pews' prescribed syllabus. Preachers with the heart of God need not apply at their churches.

Timothy, like all preachers, should not be surprised at the growth of evil in the Church. We should not be alarmed when people consciously "turn away their ears from the truth" and willingly buy into the devil's lies (v. 5). The time is coming, and now is when people graciously accept a lie rather than the truth, poison rather than the antidote, godlessness rather than godliness.

> The time is coming, and now is when people graciously accept a lie rather than the truth, poison rather than the antidote, godlessness rather than godliness.

We are closer to the end of time than Timothy was, and there has been a proliferation of evil like we have never seen before—both inside and outside the church. Far more people today do not want to hear about Jesus Christ being "the only way to God." They do not want to hear about Christ being "the way, the truth, and the life." Many people don't want to hear that the road to the Father is through the Son. They would rather believe the lie that there are many roads that lead to the Heavenly Father.

People today want to be told that Jesus Christ is *not* the Son of God. And they want to hear and believe that God would *not* stoop to co-mingle with His creation through His Son. It is easier for people to believe that Jesus was just another prophet among many. As a result, they deny Christ's virgin birth, His sacrificial death, and the resurrection for the atonement of sins. Many, however, accept the historical Jesus, but not this Jesus who declares, and has proven Himself to be Savior of the world.

Further, people don't want to be held to the standards God has set in His Word. They are the standards for all men, women, boys, and girls. There are no alternatives, no options, and no room for debate. God's Word is what it is.

Today people gleefully subscribe to horoscopes. They earnestly seek out teachers who read palms or give tarot card readings. The popularity of teachers who so-call contact the dead is on the rise, so much so, that they are now able to have their own television programs.

Today people seek out teachers who offer self-help advice that is contrary to God's Word. They are inclined to follow television talk show hosts, motivational gurus, athletes, or movie stars, rather than the Star of David.

> A generation will arise that will care less about sin, less about righteousness, less about eternal life, less about the things of God.

Paul warns Timothy and us today that a generation will arise that will care less about sin, less about righteousness, less about eternal life, less about the things of God. Therefore—none of us should be surprised—we must simply follow Paul's advice, which is to preach, the word— to reprove, rebuke, and to exhort. As living epistles, we all can make a difference. We all can preach by letting our lights shine brightly among men, while the time is still right, and day has not given over to night.

SUCCESS IN AND OUT OF THE PULPIT

Finally, Paul concludes by reminding Timothy that no matter what happens, doing his job is of the utmost importance. Therefore, "watch thou in all things, endure afflictions, do the work of an evangelist, make full proof of thy ministry" (v. 5). By following Paul's advice, Timothy would be assured of success in and out of the pulpit. As a matter of fact, the fulfillment of these four admonitions would guarantee any servant a congratulatory, "Well done."

First, Timothy is told to "watch thou in all things" better translated "be sober in all things." To be sober is the very opposite of drunkenness. Timothy is encouraged to maintain his balance in the midst of a wicked society. He must remain steadfast, unmovable, sober, and steady in the things of God.

Whether people are intoxicated with the lies of false teachers, current fads, or other crazes, the man of God must remain "sober in all things." He must remain faithful to his calling. Whether congregations continue to listen or turn a deaf ear to the truth, Timothy was to remain firm. When the majority is going in the wrong direction, the preacher/pastor must stay the course. When the crowd prefers entertainment to exegetical preaching, playing over praying, the preacher/pastor must not panic he must stay on course with the gospel.

If the climate inside the Church is the same as outside, Timothy must steady himself with the Word of God. He is still to preach the Word in season and out of season; he must continue to reprove, rebuke, and exhort. The servant of the Lord should never be disturbed over the triumph of evil. It's only for a short while. As David declared, "For they [evil doers] shall soon be cut down like the grass, and wither as the green herb" (Psalm 37:1 KJV).

> The servant of the Lord should never be disturbed over the triumph of evil. It's only for a short while.

Even when everyone else is drunk with the wine of the world, pleasing their own selfish desires by denying the power of God, both the pulpit and the pew must continue to "watch thou in all things." The church, therefore, must never give in to the things of this world because "a friend of the world is an enemy of God."

Then secondly, Paul advises Timothy and us to endure afflictions. These words come from a man who had suffered greatly for the cause of Christ (2 Corinthians 11:24ff). The followers of the Lord should not be surprised when persecution prevails. God has said, "Many are the afflictions of the righteous, but the Lord delivereth him out of them all." And "Blessed are they which are persecuted for righteousness' sake: for theirs is the kingdom of heaven" (Psalm 34:19, Matthew 6:10 KJV).

Timothy was to be prepared for whatever devices the devil used against him; and as a faithful servant of the gospel, he had to faithfully endure evil attacks and outbursts. The preacher/pastor is not to deplete his energies fighting fire with fire. Every preacher must endure the whispering, the gossips, the backbiting, and the distrust by members and non-members.

> Every preacher must endure the whispering, the gossips, the backbiting, and the distrust by members and non-members.

Many times, however, suffering can make a person think they are in it alone. Timothy was not alone, nor was he the first servant to face persecution. And, of course, he would not be the last. Most of the Master's men were persecuted. Some even met with violent deaths. The pastor/preacher, nonetheless, must endure.

Moses endured the murmuring of his people (Exodus 16:7). *Joseph* suffered at the hands of his own brothers (Genesis 37:4). *Jeremiah* was beaten and thrown in prison (Jeremiah. 20:2). *Daniel* was thrown into the lions' den (Daniel 6). *John the Baptist* was beheaded for his preaching. And *Jesus Christ*, the chief sufferer, endured at the hands of evil men (Matthew 26).

Further Paul commands, "Do the work of an evangelist." Evangelism calls for further outreach. The pastor/preacher is responsible for the local flock, as well as trying to evangelize those who have yet to hear the gospel. Paul encourages Timothy to devote himself to evangelism, a work which helps ward off false teachers and corrupt clergy that have access to the gullible and weak sheep. He was to boldly spread the Word of God far and wide by doing the work of an evangelist. Lastly, the young preacher was to "make full proof of his ministry."

In other words, Timothy was to perform his duties teaching and preaching to the best of his ability. And through his good works, Jesus would be lifted, sin would be defeated, and God glorified. Anything short of what Paul has charged Timothy to do would mean he was *not* doing his job.

Today, there is a great deal of kingdom work yet to be done. Like Timothy, we have no time to waste. We must declare God's truths while people are still hungry and thirsty for righteousness. Whatever it takes, we must be willing to endure; because, in the end, we will have to make full proof of our individual ministries. We will have to give account at His appearing.

In conclusion, we all must do our jobs and do them well if we expect to hear the Lord Jesus say, "Well done thy good and faithful servant."

> We all must do our jobs and do them well if we expect to hear the Lord Jesus say, "Well done thy good and faithful servant."

NOTES

NOTES

TODAY IS ALL
WE HAVE

At night, we retire with the expectation of witnessing a brand-new day: tomorrow.

Yet, there is no guarantee that we will see tomorrow. There is no guarantee that any of us will see another day. Today is all we have.

> We are not owed today, and we are certainly not promised tomorrow. Today is a gift, a gift from God.

Therefore, it is not wise to take today for granted. We are not owed today, and we are certainly not promised tomorrow. Today is a gift, a gift from God.

How we are to respond to *today*, this oftentimes neglected gift, is found in the Word of God.

The Word of God reveals

the kind of attitude we should have about today and how our today should shape our view of tomorrow.

Scripture teaches us of the fragility of life—how it is uncertain, fleeting, and momentary. Throughout the Word, we are reminded that we are but "dust."

> Between man and death, there is only a step (1 Samuel 20:4 NIV).

Man is a "passing breeze that does not return" (Psalms 78:39 NIV). He will "shrivel up like a leaf" (Isaiah 64:6 NIV). And between man and death, there is only a step (1 Samuel 20:4 NIV). Scripture clearly reveals that today is temporary and tentative.

Another prominent and widely quoted reminder of the kind of attitude we should have toward today comes from the epistle of James. James was the brother of the Lord and the leader of the early Church. His comments were made to a group of individuals who had a narrow perspective of life and therefore did not appreciate or regard the uncertainty of today or tomorrow. James warned:

> *Now listen, you who say, "Today or tomorrow we will go to this or that city, spend a year there, carry on business and make money." Why, you do not even know what will happen tomorrow? What is your life? You are a mist that appears for a little while and then vanishes. Instead, you ought to say, "If it is the Lord's will, we will live and do this or that." As it is, you boast and brag. All such boasting is evil.* (James 4:13-16 NIV)

James counsels everyone to be cautious about today. We have today, and we are to use it wisely. As for tomorrow, who knows?

James argued further that getting and gaining should *not* be the primary thrust of daily existence because it breeds ingratitude for the moment and can potentially poison the future.

Jesus Christ also warned about handling the cares and concerns of today and leaving tomorrow to itself. He said, "Do not worry about tomorrow, for tomorrow will worry about itself. Each day has enough troubles of its own" (Matthew 6:34 NIV).

Even the sinner is cautioned and encouraged to respond to the voice of God *today* because tomorrow is not promised: "Today, if you hear his voice, do not harden your heart" (Hebrew 4:7 NKJV).

James wisely concluded that our existence today and what today brings are based solely on the will of God: "If it is the Lord's will, we will live and do this or that." We do not control our today or God's tomorrow—*both are in His hands.*

Solomon also made this fact clear when he penned, "Boast not thyself of tomorrow; for thou knowest not what a day may bring forth" (Proverbs 27:1 KJV)

Consider for a moment the Parable of the Rich Fool in Luke 12. It is a disturbing example of one who improperly used his today to boast about a tomorrow over which he had no control. He built barns to store all of his goods and with a hearty heart believed time was on his side. The parable goes:

> *The ground of a certain rich man brought forth plentifully: And he thought within himself, saying, "What shall I do, because I have no room where to bestow my fruits?" And he said, "This will I do: I will pull down my barns, and build greater; and there will I bestow all my fruits and my goods. And I will say to my soul, Soul, thou hast much goods laid up for many years; take thine ease, eat, drink, and be merry." But God said unto him, "Thou fool, this night thy soul shall be required of thee: then whose shall those things*

be, which thou hast provided?" So is he that layeth up treasure for himself, and is not rich toward God. (Luke 12:16-21 KJV)

The rich fool learned in a most dramatic fashion that today was all he actually had. As a matter of fact, it was his last today. For on the night of the very same day, it was required of him to return to God his most valuable possession, his soul.

All our lives are but gifts from God to be used for His glory *today* and then returned, often without notice.

Remember: *today* is all we have. Yesterday has been filed on the hard drives of the past, and tomorrow is still in the hands of God, awaiting His command to be uploaded.

Therefore, enjoy today,

> appreciate today,
> please God today,
> love today,
> forgive today,
> confess today,
> rejoice today,
> and pray today.

Today is all we have. Yesterday has been filed on the hard drives of the past, and tomorrow is still in the hands of God, awaiting His command to be uploaded.

Tomorrow is not promised. Today is all we have.

NOTES

NOTES

DON'T WASTE
YOUR TIME

After class, one of my students took a seat behind me as I sat reviewing the portfolios of my colleagues. He, like the other thirty plus students, had taken his test and placed it on the desk in front of me. However, unlike the other students, who quietly left, this young man stayed behind.

When I got to a stopping point, I acknowledged his presence and asked him what more I could do for him. I thought he wanted to discuss his grades or ask a question about the test. To my delight, he responded by saying, "I want to ask you a question about the Bible."

At first, he began by voicing a concern rather than asking a question. He said that he and a group of his friends had stayed up most of the night discussing the Bible, arguing over its validity, and questioning certain aspects of Scripture. Then he asked, "What do I do when people refuse to believe, refuse to accept the truth of God's Word, and are just stubborn and close-minded to truth?"

I told him there is not very much he can do. He should simply do as Jesus did, which is to lay the truth out there and leave the rest up to God. Further, I stressed that just because he had stayed up the better part of the night discussing God's Word and trying to convince others about what God has clearly expressed in His Word was no indication that he had spent his time wisely.

> Many people will try to justify their disinterest in the Bible and their ungodly way of life by challenging your life.

Some people, young and old alike, student or non-student, are not seeking *knowledge* and *understanding*. Many people will try to justify their disinterest in the Bible and their ungodly way of life by challenging your life.

Oftentimes, this is done by luring you into unfruitful and endless discussions that go nowhere. Thus, my advice to my student, as was the apostle Paul's to young Timothy, was, "Don't waste your time" (1 Timothy 1:4)

The student seemed to find my comments rather surprising. However, I went on to explain that it is true that "silence is golden" when properly employed. You can speak volumes without speaking.

Solomon taught that there is "a time to be silent and a time to speak," (Ecclesiastes 3:7b) and in order to know which is best, one must be led by the Holy Spirit. Lengthy discussions are not clear indicators that others are convinced of what has been said.

It is our duty as Christians to share the Word with others. Yet, we must always do so in accordance with the Spirit. He will give us discernment that will enable us to know when to

> "Silence is golden" when properly employed. You can speak volumes without speaking.

move on, when to shut up, and when to continue hammering home the Word to others.

It is only when we allow the Spirit to operate through us and speak to us that we will know exactly how to respond to others.

Finally, I cited two Scriptures that I have clung to through the years to my inquisitive student. The first is found in Proverbs and the other in Matthew. Of course, there are many other Scriptures, but in Proverbs, we are told that *words are ineffective when spoken to a fool.* In other words, a word of wisdom is wasted on a fool.

More specifically, Scripture states, "Do not speak to a fool, for he will scorn the wisdom of your words" (Proverbs 23:9 NIV). The Word of God pulls no punches, and at times, it can be brutally honest. Talking all night to the fool-hearted about the Word of God, according to the Word of God, is a waste.

> Jesus makes it plain that the high and holy things of God should not be taken lightly.

The second passage was spoken by Jesus: "Give not that which is holy unto the dogs, neither cast your pearls before swine" (Matthew 7:6 KJV), Here, Jesus makes it plain that the high and holy things of God should not be taken lightly.

Jesus taught that there are those who do not take seriously the Word of God, the pearl of great price, and no matter how late at night you stay up trying to convince them, like swine, they will trample what you have said under their feet.

My advice is to always be led by the Holy Spirit whenever a discussion about the Bible ensues. The Spirit will give you discernment. If you are to speak, He will tell you what to say. If you are to speak, He will tell you how long. If you are to speak, He will even reveal to whom.

On the other hand, the Spirit may also say, "Don't waste your time."

NOTES

NOTES

PASTOR'S PRAYER

THANK YOU, LORD

For my family: for all you are doing, for all You
have done, and for all You're going to do.

THANK YOU, LORD

For my church family You have assigned me to
feed with knowledge and understanding.

THANK YOU, LORD

For my work family which is in the business
of educating your people.

FINALLY, THANK YOU LORD

For the strangers you send into my life.
May they see You in me, and come to know You, and confess You.

THANK YOU, LORD!

ABOUT THE AUTHOR

DR. CLARENCE TALLEY SR. is Senior Pastor at Mount Corinth Missionary Baptist Church, Heavenly Hempstead, Texas a fellowship that he has been affiliated with for over four decades. He is Professor of Art at Prairie View A & M University in Prairie View, Texas where he has taught, mentored, and inspired students to achieve for almost fifty years.

He received a B.A. from Southern University, an M.F.A. from Louisiana State University, an M.A. from Houston Graduate School of Theology, and a D.B.S. from Master's International School of Divinity.

Dr. Talley is a Fulbright-Hays Scholar to Africa where he has traveled East and West Africa. He is also a Phelps-Stoke Fellow to the Caribbean. His travels subsequently led to photographic essays, exhibitions/exhibit catalogues, and journal articles.

He is listed in "250 Years of Afro American Art," "Who's Who in the South and Southwest," "Who's Who Among African Americans," "Who's Who Among America's Teachers and Who's Who in Black Houston."

As an accomplished artist, Dr. Talley art works have been shown both nationally and internationally in numerous one man and group exhibitions such as The Corcoran Gallery, Washington D.C.; Black Creativity, Chicago, Illinois; Huntsville Museum of Art, Museum of Art, Port Au Prince; University of West Indies in Trinidad; Biblical Art Center, Dallas, TX, The Apex Museum, Atlanta, Georgia, University of Texas, Texas A & M, Prairie View A & M and recently in Shanghai, China and India

He is the author of Seven Things God Hates, Jesus Christ Made Straight A's, From the Pulpit to the Streets, Lie after Lie after Lie, Cruising with Jonah, A Call from God, God in the Land of Ghana, and other noted works.

Dr. Talley and his wife of 51 years, Carolyn Ann, reside in Precious Prairie View, Texas. They are the proud parents of Clarence Jr. and Crystal Ann.

OTHER BOOKS BY DR. TALLEY

Books by Clarence Talley, Sr. from Westbow Press
Cruising with Jonah: Bible Study Commentary
Seven Things God Hates:
A Biblical Perspective on Righteous Hates

Other Books by Clarence Talley, Sr.
The Call for the Prophet
A Call from God
Is It True: Reflections from the Word of God
Lie after Lie after Lie: A Study in 2 Kings 5
God in the Land of Ghana: He's Everywhere
Jesus Christ Made Straight A's

To contact Clarence Talley, Sr., write:

Clarence Talley, Sr.
P.O. Box 2134
Prairie View, TX 77446

www.clarencetalley.com
clarencetalley@att.net

Printed in the United States
by Baker & Taylor Publisher Services